Stories in English

for Beginners

Daria Galek

While every precaution has been taken in the preparation of this book, the publisher assumes no responsibility for errors or omissions, or for damages resulting from the use of the information contained herein.

STORIES IN ENGLISH FOR BEGINNERS

First edition. June 27, 2024.

ISBN: 979-8224782710

Written by Daria Galek.

Table of Contents

Introduction

Welcome to the book "Stories in English for Beginners." This unique collection contains 40 carefully selected stories to help you learn English. After each story, you'll find exercises with answers to help reinforce the knowledge you've gained.

The stories in this book vary in themes and levels of difficulty, but all are tailored to the beginner level. You'll find everyday stories as well as more exciting adventures. Each story aims to develop your knowledge of English in an enjoyable and engaging way.

The exercises accompanying each story are designed to test your understanding of the text and help you learn new words and grammatical structures. Thanks to these exercises, you will be able to systematically develop your language skills.

I hope this book becomes for you not only a learning tool but also a source of joy and satisfaction in discovering a new language.

Good luck and happy reading!

Tips for Reading Stories in English

Reading stories in English can be both enjoyable and highly effective in learning a new language. To fully benefit from the stories in this book, it's worth applying a few simple but effective strategies. Here are some tips that might help you:

1. **Read aloud**: Reading aloud helps improve pronunciation and fluency. You'll hear how words and sentences sound, which is extremely helpful in learning a foreign language.

2. **Don't be afraid to make mistakes**: Learning a new language is a process where making mistakes is natural and inevitable. Every mistake is an opportunity to learn and improve.

3. **Focus on understanding the overall meaning**: At first, you don't need to understand every word. Concentrate on grasping the overall meaning of the story. Over time, you'll understand more details.

4. **Use a dictionary**: If you find difficult words, use a dictionary to look up their meaning. This will help you expand your vocabulary effectively.

5. **Take notes**: Write down new words and phrases you encounter while reading. This way, you can revisit them and reinforce your knowledge.

6. **Complete the exercises after each story**: Exercises are a key element of learning. Solve them carefully to check your understanding of the text and reinforce new vocabulary and grammatical structures.

7. **Read regularly**: Regularity is the key to success in language learning. Try to read every day, even if it's just for a few minutes. Regular reading will help you gradually develop your language skills.

8. **Re-read**: Don't be afraid to go back to stories you've already read. Re-reading will help you better understand the text and reinforce new words and grammatical structures.

9. **Use context**: If you encounter a difficult word, try to guess its meaning based on the context. This is a skill that will be very useful in language learning.

10. **Be patient**: Learning a language is a process that takes time. Be patient and consistent, and you will definitely see progress.

Remember, learning a language is not just about gaining knowledge, but also about enjoying the discovery of a new culture and ways of expression.

Chapter 1. Day at School

Emma woke up early, just like every morning. She quickly got dressed and went to the dining room for breakfast. Her mother had already prepared toast with jam and a glass of warm milk.

"Hurry up, Emma! You don't want to be late for school again," her mother said as she cleared the dishes.

Emma nodded and put her books in her backpack. She left the house and walked a few blocks to the school. In the playground, some of her friends were already playing.

The bell rang, and all the children lined up to enter the building. The first class was math. Emma paid close attention as the teacher explained addition and subtraction on the board.

Afterward, they had a recess. Emma and her friends played hopscotch and ate a small snack.

The next classes were reading and natural sciences. Emma really enjoyed learning about animals and plants.

When the dismissal bell rang, Emma gathered her things and headed to the main door. Her mother was already waiting for her to walk home together.

Chapter 2. A Walk in the Park

Olivia and her mom left the house and walked towards the nearby park. It was a sunny and hot day. The park was full of people enjoying the nice weather.

They saw little children playing on the swings and running on the soft, green grass. Birds were singing cheerful songs among the branches of tall trees. Brightly colored flowers adorned the park's pathways.

Mom pointed to a squirrel climbing up the rough trunk of a large oak tree. "Look at that squirrel, Olivia!" she said with a smile. Olivia watched with wide eyes as the small animal moved nimbly.

They continued walking and reached a fountain with clear water. Olivia took some coins from her pocket and tossed them into the water, closing her eyes to make a wish. Then, they continued exploring the corners of the park.

They saw butterflies flitting from flower to flower, sipping the sweet nectar. The scent of spring flowers filled the fresh air. In the top of a leafy tree, they spotted a bird's nest among the branches. Mom quietly explained to Olivia that they should walk silently so as not to scare the birds. Olivia nodded, amazed by the natural beauty surrounding them.

Chapter 3. Shopping at the Supermarket

William needed to buy some things for his new apartment. He went to the supermarket near his house.

When he entered, he took a shopping cart. First, he went to the fruits and vegetables aisle. He saw many fresh options. He chose some red apples, yellow bananas, and orange carrots. He put them in the cart.

Then he moved to the meat section. He saw chicken, beef, and sausages. He decided to take some chicken and a few sausages to make simple meals. He added them to the cart.

Next, he went to the dairy products aisle. He picked up a carton of milk, a pack of cheese, and a strawberry yogurt. He continued walking through the supermarket.

In the bakery aisle, he saw freshly baked bread. He chose a whole grain loaf and some sweet buns. He carefully placed them in the cart.

When he had finished buying everything he needed, he headed to the checkout lanes. There was a long line, but it moved quickly. When it was his turn, he put all the items on the conveyor belt.

The cashier scanned each product. William paid with his debit card. The cashier handed him the bags with his purchases.

William left the supermarket happy to have successfully completed his shopping.

Chapter 4. Liam's Family

Liam has a small but happy family. In his house live his dad Noah, his mom Ava, his sister Sophia, and his grandmother Abigail.

Noah is tall and has short black hair. He is a hardworking and responsible man. Besides cooking, he likes fixing things around the house. He is always willing to help others. In his free time, he enjoys watching soccer games on television.

Ava is kind and loving, and she is always ready to listen to her children. Besides being a teacher, she is an excellent cook and often prepares delicious recipes for the family. She likes gardening and teaching her children about nature.

Sophia is a very energetic and curious girl. She is always ready to explore and discover new things. She loves drawing and doing crafts. She is very creative, and her parents are always surprised by her innovative ideas.

Abigail is the heart of the family. She always has a smile on her face and wise advice to give. Besides baking cookies, she likes knitting and crocheting. Her grandchildren love listening to her stories about the past and learning from her experience.

Together, they form a strong and united team that faces challenges and celebrates the joys of life.

Chapter 5. James's Birthday

James is very excited because today is his birthday. He is turning seven and wants to celebrate with his school friends. Since last week, he has been telling all his classmates that he is going to have a big birthday party at his house.

James's mom has been preparing everything for the celebration. She bought a big chocolate cake with frosting and candles, colorful balloons, and birthday hats. James helped decorate the living room with streamers and "Happy Birthday" signs.

When the guests arrived, James greeted them with a big smile. They all brought gifts wrapped in shiny paper. They played hide and seek, had sack races, and broke a piñata full of candies. The clown performed funny tricks and made animal balloons to entertain them.

After that, everyone sang "Happy Birthday" while James blew out the candles on the cake. He made a wish before blowing out the candles. Then, they handed out slices of cake to all the children. Each of the guests enjoyed their slice of cake with great enthusiasm.

In the end, James thanked everyone for coming and for making his day so special. He was very happy to have such amazing friends.

Chapter 6. A Day at the Beach

Mia woke up early that morning, excited to spend a day at the beach with her family. After breakfast, she packed a backpack with towels, sunscreen, and some beach toys.

When they arrived, the sun was shining brightly, and the sand was very hot. Mia and her little brother Oliver ran towards the water, laughing and splashing. Their parents spread out the beach towels and set up a big umbrella for shade.

"Come on, Mia!" Oliver shouted from the water. "It's great!"

Mia joined her brother, and they played tag and buried each other in the sand. Oliver built a small sandcastle, and Mia decorated it with shells she found.

After a while, their dad called them to eat. He took out sandwiches, fruit, and drinks from a cooler. Mia tried delicious olives and serrano ham for the first time.

"Do you like the food, Mia?" her dad asked, smiling.

"Yes, I love it!" Mia replied enthusiastically.

They spent the afternoon sunbathing, reading stories, and walking along the beach. Mia collected many beautiful shells as souvenirs. At sunset, they packed up their things and returned home, tired but happy after a lovely day at the beach.

Chapter 7. At the Train Station

Amelia and her family are going to travel by train to visit their grandparents. Amelia wakes up early and dresses in comfortable clothes, pants, and a light T-shirt.

When they arrive at the train station, there are many people walking around with suitcases and luggage. Amelia looks around excitedly, observing the large clocks showing the arrival and departure times of the trains.

Her dad approaches the counter to buy the tickets. A friendly lady in a blue uniform smiles at them and helps them choose the right seats.

After buying the tickets, the family walks to the platform where they will wait for their train. Amelia and her younger brother, Daniel, entertain themselves by counting the train cars on the track. "One, two, three, four..." they count out loud, laughing when they lose track.

Their mom, Elena, buys them some sweets at the station's kiosk. Amelia chooses some chocolate chip cookies, while Daniel prefers some sugary gummy candies. They eat their treats while they wait, savoring the sweet bites.

Suddenly, they hear a loud whistle, and the train begins to move slowly towards the platform. "Here it comes!" Amelia shouts, jumping with excitement. The family stands up, ready to board and start their exciting train journey.

Chapter 8. My Pet

My pet's name is Max. He is a very small and very cute puppy. He has short dark brown fur and big black eyes that shine brightly.

Max loves to play and run. When I come home after school, he always greets me, wagging his tail very happily. He likes to chase a red ball all over the park and brings it back for me to throw it again.

Max's favorite toy is a red plastic bone. He carries it in his mouth and takes it around the house. It's very funny to see him run with the bone and shake it to make noise. Sometimes, he even hides it under the furniture.

After playing so much, Max likes to rest. He curls up in his little bed and falls asleep right away. Sometimes he snores a little and moves his paws as if he is dreaming of chasing something.

I really like spending time with Max. He is my best friend and always gives me affection. I can't imagine life without my little four-legged companion.

Chapter 9. A Rainy Day

Today is a rainy day. Outside, the drops are falling from the sky and the ground is wet. We can't go out to play, but that doesn't mean we can't have fun inside the house.

Mom, wanting us not to get bored, took several books and board games from the shelves and placed them on the living room table. She told us we could choose something we liked and spend time reading or playing, listening to the sound of rain on the roof.

I choose a book of fairy tales and sit on the sofa with a blanket. I open the book and immerse myself in the magical stories of princesses and dragons.

My sister, Harper, prefers playing board games. We take out the chessboard and sit facing each other. She moves her pieces carefully, thinking through each move. Sometimes she wins, but I enjoy playing with her a lot.

Meanwhile, mom is in the kitchen preparing something delicious for lunch. The smell of hot soup spreads throughout the house and makes us feel happy.

That's how we spend our rainy day, amidst books, games, and comforting meals. Although we can't go outside, we are happy to be together and enjoy family time.

Chapter 10. Dinner at Home

One afternoon, Elijah's mom was getting ready to make dinner and Elijah decided to help her. He was very excited because he loves being in the kitchen.

His mom decided they were going to make a big salad, baked chicken, and vegetable rice. First, they went to the supermarket to buy the ingredients. They bought lettuce, tomatoes, carrots, and cucumbers for the salad. They also bought a fresh chicken and some vegetables for the rice.

When they got home, they started preparing dinner. Elijah washed the vegetables and carefully chopped them. His dad seasoned the chicken with salt, pepper, and a little lemon. Then, he put the chicken in the oven.

Mom cooked the rice in a large pot and added the chopped vegetables. The whole house smelled delicious as the food cooked.

After an hour, dinner was ready. The family set the table with plates, glasses, and cutlery. Elijah helped to serve the salad and the rice. Dad took the chicken out of the oven and sliced it into portions.

The whole family sat down at the table and started eating. "This tastes so good!" Elijah said with a smile. Everyone agreed and enjoyed the meal together.

Chapter 11. Visit to the Zoo

On a hot Sunday morning, Aiden and his friend Jacob decided to visit the London zoo. Aiden was very excited because he had never been to a zoo before.

Upon arrival, they bought their tickets and entered quickly. The first thing they saw were the lions, resting under the sun.

"Look how big those lions are!" exclaimed Aiden, his eyes wide open.

Next, they walked towards the area with the elephants. The huge gray pachyderms were bathing in a water pond.

"They look like walking houses!" chuckled Jacob, observing their slow and heavy movements.

Afterwards, they visited the monkey habitat. The mischievous animals were jumping from branch to branch, making funny noises.

"They look like kids playing in a park," remarked Aiden.

Later on, they went to the aviary, where they saw birds of vibrant colors flying freely. Aiden watched in fascination as the parrots with bright feathers moved around. Jacob pointed out that they looked like small flying rainbows.

At lunchtime, they ate sandwiches they had packed, sitting at a picnic area. They excitedly talked about all the fascinating animals they had seen so far.

Chapter 12. A Day in the Mountains

On a beautiful day, Logan and his family decided to go hiking in the mountains. They were excited to explore nature and enjoy the fresh air.

"Let's go, let's go! I don't want to miss anything," said Logan as he packed his backpack.

They set out early, carrying food and water in their backpacks. Logan didn't forget his camera to capture the landscapes along the way.

As they walked along the trail, Logan picked some wildflowers and admired the birds singing.

After a while, they found the perfect spot for a picnic. They sat together and enjoyed the view of the majestic mountains while sharing their food.

After the picnic, they continued their journey, marveling at the beauty of the surrounding nature.

Finally, they reached the top of a mountain and stopped to rest. Logan took out his camera and captured the breathtaking view.

"Dad, Mom, look at these incredible views!" exclaimed Logan excitedly.

"Yes, son, they are truly beautiful," replied his father with a smile.

They stayed a while longer enjoying the scenery before starting their descent, feeling grateful for the wonderful day spent together as a family.

Chapter 13. My Best Friend

My best friend's name is Alexander. We met at school and have been inseparable ever since. Alexander is tall, has brown hair, and always wears a smile on his face.

Alexander loves playing soccer, and so do I, so we spend many afternoons practicing at the park near our house. We have a lot of fun chasing after the ball and scoring goals.

When we're not playing soccer, we enjoy exploring the neighborhood in search of adventures. We often ride our bikes along the trails in the nearby forest or simply walk through the city streets, discovering new places together.

In addition to our adventures, Alexander and I love building things with building blocks. We spend hours creating castles, cities, and spaceships, letting our imagination soar.

What I value most about Alexander is that he's always there for me, in good times and bad. We can always count on each other, and that's what makes our friendship so special.

Chapter 14. The Neighborhood Party

Last night, a very fun party took place. All the neighbors gathered to celebrate together. There was a lot of music, delicious food, and dancing.

The party started at dusk when people began arriving at the park. Everyone was excited to have a good time together.

Children were playing and laughing, while adults chatted and shared stories. Soon, the food was ready and everyone lined up to serve themselves.

"Do you like samosa, Ethan? They're my specialty," Evelyn said, offering one to her neighbor.

"Of course! Thank you, Evelyn! It smells delicious," Ethan replied, taking an empanada and savoring it.

After eating, the music got louder and everyone started dancing. Dance circles formed and people moved to the rhythm of the music.

"Come on, Evelyn! Dance with me!" exclaimed Ethan, extending his hand to his neighbor.

"Sure, Ethan! I'd love to!" Evelyn responded, taking his hand and joining the dance.

The party lasted until late at night, and we all had a great time. It was a wonderful opportunity to come together as a community and celebrate friendship among neighbors.

Chapter 15. The Doctor's Visit

Last week, Thomas had to go to the doctor because he wasn't feeling well. He had a headache, fever, and cough. His dad called the doctor's office and managed to get an appointment for the same day.

When they arrived at the doctor's office, the receptionist asked them to wait in the waiting room. After a few minutes, Dr. Smith called them in. Thomas and his dad entered the examination room and sat down.

Dr. Smith asked Thomas about his symptoms. "I have a headache, fever, and a bad cough," explained Thomas.

The doctor nodded and then took Thomas's temperature. "You have a fever, but it's not very high," said the doctor. Then, he listened to Thomas's chest with a stethoscope. "Your lungs sound good, but it seems like you have a strong cold."

Dr. Smith prescribed a cough syrup for Thomas and advised him to rest a lot and drink plenty of water. He also suggested that Thomas stay home for a few days to fully recover.

Before they left, the doctor gave Thomas a lollipop for being a good patient. Thomas smiled and thanked him.

Back home, Thomas followed the doctor's instructions. He rested, took his syrup, and soon started feeling better. He was grateful for visiting the doctor and receiving the right treatment.

Chapter 16. The Soccer Match

On Saturday afternoon, Henry and his friends gathered at the park to play soccer.

Henry arrived first and marked the field with rocks and backpacks. Soon after, his friends Jackson, Sebastian, Carter, and Matthew arrived. They were very excited and full of energy.

"Let's form the teams!" said Henry eagerly.

With the teams set, they started playing.

Right from the start, the match was intense. Henry ran fast with the ball, dodging players from the other team. When he got close to the goal, Jackson passed him the ball and Henry kicked it hard. Goal! Jackson' team celebrated with joy.

"Well done, Henry!" shouted Jackson, patting him on the back.

Sebastian and Carter also played very well and tied the match. Everyone enjoyed the game a lot.

Time flew by and soon the sun was setting. They decided that the next goal would decide the winner. Both teams played with more energy and focus.

Finally, Henry managed to steal the ball, ran towards the opposing goal, and with a good shot, scored the winning goal. His team lifted him up in the air, celebrating his great play.

"We won!" shouted Matthew with a huge smile.

After the match, everyone sat on the grass, tired but happy. They shared drinks and snacks, laughing and reminiscing about the best moments of the game.

Chapter 17. My Room

My room is my favorite place in the house. It's small but very cozy. The walls are light blue, and there's a large window that lets in a lot of natural light.

In the center of the room, I have a comfortable bed with a brightly colored quilt. Next to the bed, there's a bedside table where I always keep a book and a reading lamp.

My desk is by the window. It's where I do my homework and draw. Above the desk, I have some shelves filled with books, notebooks, and my colored pencils.

Across from the bed, there's a large wardrobe where I keep my clothes and shoes. I also have a small shelf where I place my favorite toys and figures.

In one corner of the room, I have a comfortable chair where I sit to read or listen to music. Additionally, there's a corkboard on the wall where I pin up photos and important notes.

What I like most about my room is the feeling of tranquility it gives me. It's my sanctuary where I can read, study, and dream. I love spending time there because it's a place where I always feel happy and relaxed.

Chapter 18. A Plane Journey

It was Abigail's first time traveling by plane. She was excited but also a little nervous. At London airport, there was a hustle and bustle of people coming and going. Abigail and her mother stood in line to check their luggage.

"How exciting, isn't it, sweetheart?" said mom as they waited their turn. "Soon you'll be in Paris."

When their turn came, a friendly flight attendant in a white uniform checked their tickets and documents. Then they headed to the boarding gate where the plane bound for Paris awaited. Abigail sat by the window and fastened her seatbelt. She looked out eagerly through the small opening.

After a few minutes of waiting, the plane started moving along the runway. Abigail's heart was pounding. Suddenly, the aircraft gained speed and almost before she knew it, they were in the air.

"Look at those incredible views!" exclaimed Abigail, pressed against the window.

Below them, the houses and streets looked tiny like construction toys. The clouds were fluffy and white. Abigail felt like a bird soaring through the sky. After a few hours of flight, the plane descended and landed smoothly at Paris airport. Abigail and her mother were excited to begin their adventure in Paris.

Chapter 19. My Spanish Class

My Spanish class is very fun. Our teacher is Mrs. Johnson. She is very kind and always helps us when we have doubts.

In my class, there are ten students. My friends are Emily, Charlotte, Wyatt, and Scarlett. Emily is very good at grammar. Charlotte always participates in class and enjoys speaking in Spanish. Wyatt is a bit shy, but he loves learning new vocabulary. Scarlett is very good at pronunciation.

Classes are on Tuesdays and Thursdays. We always start with a game in Spanish. Then, Mrs. Johnson teaches us new words and phrases. Sometimes, we watch videos in Spanish and practice dialogues. We also read short stories and do exercises in the textbook.

I really like my Spanish class because I learn and have fun at the same time. My classmates are very friendly, and we always work together. At the end of class, we always have a little conversation in Spanish to practice what we've learned.

I am very happy to be in this class and improve my Spanish every day. I'm sure that soon I will speak Spanish fluently.

Chapter 20. The Library

On Saturday morning, John went to the library. He loves reading very much and is always looking for new books.

Upon entering, John greeted the librarian, Mrs. Grace. She is always very friendly and helps him find good books. John walked among the shelves, looking at all the titles.

First, he went to the adventure section. He found a book about pirates that caught his attention. Then, he went to the science fiction section and saw a book about space travel. John also wanted a book about animals, so he went to the nature section.

After choosing three books, John went to a table and sat down. He opened the pirate book and started reading. The story was very exciting and John couldn't stop reading. An hour passed, and John decided to take all three books home.

John went to the counter, and Mrs. Grace helped him check out the books. "Enjoy your reading, John," she said with a smile.

John left the library very happy. He couldn't wait to get home and continue reading his new books. For him, the library is a magical place where he always finds adventures and knowledge.

Chapter 21. An Afternoon at the Movies

One afternoon, Lily and her friends decided to go to the cinema. They wanted to see a new movie that everyone was saying was very good. They met at the cinema entrance at five o'clock.

First, they bought tickets at the ticket counter. After purchasing the tickets, they went to the snack shop.

In the shop, they bought popcorn, sodas, and candy. Lily chose a cola soda and a large box of popcorn. Her friends also bought popcorn and different types of candy. With their snacks in hand, they entered the movie theater.

The theater was dark, and there were many people. They found their seats and sat comfortably. The movie started, and everyone became quiet, paying close attention to the screen.

The movie was very exciting. There were many action scenes, and the special effects were impressive. Lily and her friends ate popcorn while watching the movie. Everyone was very happy and enjoyed themselves a lot.

After two hours, the movie ended. Lily and her friends left the cinema discussing their favorite scenes. Everyone agreed it was a very fun afternoon and decided to go back to the cinema soon to watch another movie.

Chapter 22. The Music Festival

Alice was very excited because she was going to attend a music festival. It was her first festival, and she couldn't wait to see her favorite bands. The festival took place in a large park, and Alice arrived early to find a good spot.

The first concert was by a rock band she really liked. Alice sang along to all the songs and enjoyed every minute. Then, she went to see a pop group. The music was upbeat, and Alice danced with her friends.

There were many other activities at the festival. Alice and her friends bought food from the stalls and tried different types of dishes. They also visited souvenir shops, and Alice bought a festival T-shirt.

At night, the festival lit up with lights and colors. The last concert was the best. The headline band played all their popular songs, and the crowd was lively. Alice felt very happy and enjoyed the show immensely.

By the end of the day, Alice was tired but very content. It was an incredible experience, and she couldn't wait to come back next year. The music festival was a day she would always cherish.

Chapter 23. A Bike Ride

Freddie and his dad decided to go for a bike ride around the city. The sun was shining, and the air was fresh. Freddie was excited to explore the area with his dad.

"Dad, where are we going today?" Freddie asked eagerly.

"We'll go to the park first and then take a ride along the river," his dad replied with a smile.

They mounted their bikes and began their adventure. Freddie enjoyed the scenery as they pedaled together. They saw tall trees, colorful flowers, and many happy people strolling around.

Suddenly, Freddie spotted a dirt road that looked interesting. "Dad, can we go there?" he asked.

"Of course, son! Let's explore," his dad replied cheerfully.

They changed direction and took the dirt road. They discovered a beautiful forest full of singing birds and small streams. Freddie was thrilled to have found such a special place.

After a while, they returned to the main path and continued their journey. Freddie felt happy to spend time with his dad and to have had so many adventures together on their bike ride.

Chapter 24. Art Class

Julia was excited because today was art class. She loved painting and creating new things. Their teacher, Mrs. White, always had interesting ideas for them.

When Julia arrived in the classroom, she saw many paintings and brushes on the tables. Mrs. White smiled and said, "Today we are going to paint a landscape. Think of your favorite place and paint what you see."

Julia thought of the beach she visited with her family. She picked up her brushes and began painting the sea, the sand, and the palm trees. She was very focused and happy.

Her friend Lucy, who was sitting next to her, looked over and said, "Julia, your painting is very beautiful!"

Julia smiled and replied, "Thank you, Lucy. I'm painting the beach where I go with my family."

The class went by quickly, and all the students created beautiful landscapes. Mrs. White walked among the tables, admiring everyone's work.

"Very well, Julia! I really like your painting. Do you enjoy painting?" the teacher asked.

"Yes, I love painting," Julia said with a big smile.

At the end of the class, everyone showed their paintings. Julia was very proud of her artwork and couldn't wait for the next art class.

Chapter 25. A Snowy Day

David woke up and looked out the window. Everything was covered in snow! He was very excited. He put on his coat, gloves, scarf, and hat. Then, he went out into the garden to play.

First, David made snowballs. He threw some at a tree and laughed a lot. Then, he decided to build a snowman. He gathered a lot of snow and started rolling a big ball for the body. Next, he made a smaller ball for the head.

David searched for rocks to use as the snowman's eyes. He also used a carrot for the nose and an old scarf for the neck. The snowman looked very nice.

While he was working, his friend Jack arrived. "Hi, David! Can I help you with the snowman?" Jack asked.

"Of course, Jack! Let's finish it together," David replied with a smile.

The two friends placed some buttons on the snowman to make the mouth. Then, they found two branches for the arms. Finally, they put a hat on the snowman's head.

As the sun began to set, David and Jack went inside the house. David's mom gave them hot chocolate to warm up. "Thank you, Mom," said David, happy and tired.

Chapter 26. The History Museum

Benjamin visited the history museum with his class. They were very excited to learn new things. Their teacher, Mr. Jones, guided them through the museum.

First, Mr. Jones took them to the dinosaur room. There were large dinosaur skeletons. Benjamin looked in awe at the enormous bones.

"These dinosaurs lived millions of years ago," explained Mr. Jones. "Did you know that Tyrannosaurus Rex was one of the largest?"

Next, they went to the ancient Egyptian room. They saw mummies and sarcophagi. Benjamin was fascinated by the stories of pharaohs and pyramids.

"The pyramids were tombs for the pharaohs," said Mr. Jones. "The Egyptians believed in life after death."

Then, they visited the Middle Ages room. There were knights' armor and swords. Benjamin imagined himself as a brave knight fighting battles.

"In the Middle Ages, castles were very important," explained Mr. Jones. "They served as fortresses and homes for nobles."

At the end of the tour, they went to the modern history room. They saw objects from the 19th and 20th centuries, like old cars and antique telephones.

Benjamin learned a lot during his visit to the museum. At the end of the day, he was happy and told his parents everything he had seen and learned.

Chapter 27. My Favorite Breakfast

My favorite breakfast is very simple and delicious. I like to prepare a vegan breakfast every morning. First, I take a banana and slice it into rounds. Then, I put the slices in a bowl. Sometimes, I use two bananas if I'm very hungry.

Next, I add some fresh strawberries and blueberries. I love fruits because they are very healthy and taste great. Then, I sprinkle some oats over the fruits. I enjoy oats because they keep me full longer.

To make the breakfast more special, I add a tablespoon of almond butter. I really like almond butter because it's creamy and delicious. Sometimes, I also sprinkle some chia seeds on top.

Finally, I pour in some almond milk. I prefer almond milk because it's vegan and has a smooth flavor. It also gives a creamy texture to the breakfast.

I sit down at the table and enjoy my breakfast. It's very nutritious and gives me a lot of energy to start the day. This breakfast is my favorite because it's easy to prepare and very tasty.

Chapter 28. A Day in the Countryside

Megan woke up early and was very excited. Today, she was going to the countryside with her family. She put on comfortable clothes and packed a backpack with water and snacks.

When they arrived at the countryside, Megan saw many animals. There were cows, sheep, and horses. Megan was happy to see so many animals. She approached a cow and petted it. "It's so soft!" Megan said with a big smile.

Afterward, Megan and her family walked along a trail in the forest. The trees were tall, and there were many colorful flowers. The air was fresh and clean. Megan took a deep breath and felt really good.

At noon, they sat under a large tree for lunch. They ate sandwiches and fresh fruits. While they ate, they listened to the birds singing. It was a very beautiful sound.

After lunch, Megan played with her little brother. They ran around the field and picked flowers. Megan made a flower crown and put it on her head. She felt like a queen of the countryside.

At the end of the day, Megan and her family returned home. Megan was tired but very happy. She had a wonderful day in the countryside, surrounded by animals and nature. "I could live there," Megan thought as she fell asleep.

Chapter 29. The Dentist Visit

Charlie had an appointment with the dentist. He was a little scared because he didn't like pain. His mom reassured him that everything would be fine and that the dentist was very friendly.

When they arrived at the clinic, they sat in the waiting room. Charlie saw magazines and some toys. He tried to relax by playing with a toy car.

"Charlie, the dentist is ready to see you," said the nurse with a smile.

Charlie entered the dentist's office. The dentist, Dr. Davis, greeted him. "Hello, Charlie. Don't worry, we'll quickly check your teeth," Dr. Davis said.

Charlie sat in the big chair. Dr. Davis explained everything he was going to do. He examined his teeth with a small mirror and a light.

"Your teeth are in great shape, Charlie. You just need to brush them better at night," Dr. Davis said.

Charlie felt relieved. The dentist didn't do anything painful. "Thank you, doctor," Charlie said with a smile.

After the check-up, Dr. Davis gave Charlie a new toothbrush and a small tube of toothpaste. "Remember to brush your teeth twice a day and use dental floss," he advised.

Charlie and his mom left the clinic. "Visiting the dentist wasn't so bad," Charlie thought. He was glad he had taken good care of his teeth.

Chapter 30. The Book Fair

Steve went to the book fair with his mother. He was very excited because he loves books. The fair was in a large park, and there were many book stalls.

"Let's find some new books for you," said his mother with a smile.

First, they went to a children's book stall. There were many books with bright colors and beautiful illustrations. Steve saw a book about dinosaurs and picked it up. "Mom, I want this book," he said excitedly.

"Of course, Steve. Do you want to look at other books too?" his mother asked.

They continued walking around the fair. Steve found an adventure book that he also liked a lot. "Mom, can I have this one too?" he asked.

"Yes, you can have both," his mother replied. "It's important to read and learn new things."

After buying the books, Steve and his mother sat on a bench. Steve started reading his new dinosaur book. He was very happy and enjoyed the book fair a lot.

"I love the book fair," said Steve. "I want to come back next year."

His mother smiled and said, "Of course, Steve. Reading is a great adventure."

Chapter 31. A Walk Downtown

Mike decided to spend the afternoon downtown. He put on his jacket and left home. The sun was shining, and the weather was nice.

First, Mike walked through the streets filled with shops. He looked at the store windows and saw many interesting things. He went into a clothing store and bought a new T-shirt.

After that, Mike visited a bookstore. He loves reading, so he spent a lot of time looking for an interesting book. Finally, he found one about adventures and bought it.

As he was leaving, Mike saw his friend Noah. "Hi, Noah! What are you doing here?" Mike asked.

"Hi, Mike. I'm looking for a gift for my sister. And you?" Noah replied.

"I just bought an adventure book," Mike said with a smile.

Then, Mike went to a café. He ordered a coffee and a chocolate cake. He sat by the window and enjoyed his snack while watching people pass by.

Lastly, Mike decided to visit a museum. There was a modern art exhibition. He walked through the halls and admired the paintings and sculptures.

At the end of the day, Mike felt happy and satisfied. As he walked home, he thought about how nice it had been to spend time exploring.

Chapter 32. A Day at the Aquarium

Kate and her classmates decided to go to the aquarium on a school trip. They were excited to see the fish and other sea creatures. When they arrived at the aquarium, they went straight to the large tanks filled with colorful fish.

"Look how beautiful they are!" exclaimed Kate, pointing to the swimming fish.

Her friends nodded excitedly and began naming the different types of fish they saw. They spent a lot of time admiring the tanks and watching the fish move.

After seeing the fish, they went to an area where they could touch starfish and sea urchins. Kate was surprised to feel how soft some of these creatures were.

"This is so amazing!" said Kate as she touched a starfish.

They ended their visit with a presentation about sharks. Kate and her friends sat together and listened attentively as they learned about the different types of sharks and how they behave in the ocean.

At the end of the day, Kate and her friends were exhausted but happy. They had had an incredible day at the aquarium, full of exciting discoveries and memorable experiences.

Chapter 33. The New Year's Eve Party

The New Year's Eve party was about to begin. Miley and Andrew were very excited. They had invited their friends to their house to celebrate together.

"This year is going to be amazing!" said Miley as she decorated the living room with garlands and balloons. Andrew was setting up the music and lights.

At ten o'clock, their friends started to arrive. Nicole, Tyler, Susan, and Justin came with food and drinks. "Happy New Year in advance!" said Susan as she hugged Miley.

Everyone sat at the table and enjoyed a delicious dinner. "The food is delicious, Miley," said Tyler. After dinner, they started dancing and laughing.

There were only a few minutes left until midnight. Everyone gathered in front of the television to watch the countdown. "Ten, nine, eight...!" they counted out loud. At midnight, everyone ate their grapes and hugged. "Happy New Year!" they shouted. Then they went out to the garden to watch the fireworks.

Miley and Andrew were very happy to have spent such a special New Year's Eve with their friends. "This is going to be a great year," said Andrew as he hugged Miley.

Chapter 34. Music Class

Sarah was very excited about her music class. She really enjoyed learning to play instruments. Today, her teacher, Mr. Moore, was going to teach them how to play the flute.

"Good morning, class," said Mr. Moore. "Today we're going to learn how to play the flute. Everyone, take a flute from the table."

Sarah took her flute and sat in her chair. Mr. Moore showed them how to hold the flute and how to blow to make a sound.

"First, we place our fingers here and here," explained Mr. Moore, pointing to the holes on the flute. "Then, we blow gently."

Sarah tried to follow the instructions. At first, she couldn't make any sound, but Mr. Moore helped her.

"Try again, Sarah," said Mr. Moore. "Remember to blow gently."

Sarah tried again, and this time, she made a sound. She was very happy.

"Very good, Sarah!" said Mr. Moore. "Now, let's learn a simple song."

Mr. Moore played a song on his flute, and the students imitated him. Sarah practiced a lot and gradually improved. By the end of the class, all the students were able to play the song.

Sarah was very proud of what she had learned. "I love music class," she thought as she put away her flute.

Chapter 35. The New Job

On his first day at the new job, Daniel was very nervous. He got up early, put on his best suit, and prepared his briefcase. He had a quick breakfast, mentally reviewing everything he needed to bring.

After arriving at the office, he was greeted by his new boss, Mr. Wilson. "Welcome, Daniel," said Mr. Wilson with a friendly smile. Daniel felt a bit more relaxed.

During the morning, Daniel learned about his tasks and how to use the company's system. Sandra, a coworker, showed him how to enter data into the computer. "Here you need to enter your username and password," explained Sandra. Daniel nodded, focused. "Thanks, Sandra," he said.

In the afternoon, he worked on his first project. He felt a bit lost at first. Sandra noticed his difficulty and came over to help him. "It's in the project folder, here," she said, pointing to the screen. "Ah, I see. Thanks again," Daniel said, relieved.

At the end of the day, Mr. Wilson approached Daniel. "Good job, Daniel. I'm sure you'll be a great member of the team," he said. Daniel went home tired but happy, knowing that in time he would feel more comfortable in his new job.

Chapter 36. A Day at the Gym

Alex woke up early in the morning with a determination in mind: he was going to start taking care of his health and fitness. He decided that today would be the day he joined the gym in his neighborhood.

After having a nutritious breakfast, he dressed in sportswear and headed to the gym. Upon entering, he felt a little nervous but also excited to begin this new phase in his life.

A friendly instructor greeted him and guided him around the gym, showing him the different machines and training equipment. Alex felt a bit overwhelmed at first, but the instructor explained how to use each machine safely and effectively.

He decided to start with a light warm-up on the treadmill. Then, he moved on to lifting weights and doing strength exercises.

After an hour of intense training, Alex felt tired but satisfied. He knew he had taken a big step toward his goal of being fit and healthy.

As he left the gym, he promised himself to keep going regularly. He was excited to see the positive changes that would come with his new exercise routine.

Chapter 37. The Photography Workshop

Camila had always been interested in photography, so when she saw an advertisement for photography workshops in her neighborhood, she decided to sign up immediately.

On the first day of the workshop, Camila was a bit nervous but excited to learn something new. With her camera in hand, she arrived at the venue and was greeted by the instructor, who welcomed her with a kind smile.

During the class, Camila learned the basics of photography, such as composition, exposure, and focus. They practiced taking photos in different locations and lighting conditions.

As the class progressed, Camila felt more confident and enthusiastic about her progress. She began capturing creative images and experimenting with different angles and perspectives. She discovered that she particularly enjoyed photographing nature and the small details that often went unnoticed.

"Great job, Camila!" exclaimed the instructor upon seeing one of her photos. "You captured the moment beautifully and naturally."

Camila felt very happy and proud. At that moment, she knew she loved photography and wanted to explore the world with her camera. She imagined traveling to distant places, taking beautiful photos, and learning about different cultures.

Chapter 38. The Dance Class

Gary had always wanted to learn how to dance, so he decided to enroll in a dance class in his neighborhood. On the first day of class, he was a bit nervous but very excited.

When he arrived at the dance studio, he was greeted by the teacher, Mrs. Miller. "Hello, welcome to our dance class," she said with a smile.

Gary joined the other students and the class began. Mrs. Miller taught them the basic steps of salsa. "First, we move the right foot forward, then the left foot back," she explained.

At first, Gary felt a bit clumsy, but with practice, he started to feel more confident. The music was lively, and everyone in the class was having a great time.

"Very good, Gary!" said Mrs. Miller. "You're improving with each step."

After an hour of practice, Gary and his classmates danced a small choreography together. Gary felt very happy and proud of his progress.

At the end of the class, Mrs. Miller gave them some tips for practicing at home. Gary left the studio tired, but very happy and eager to continue learning how to dance.

Chapter 39. The First Day of Vacation

Brad was very excited about the start of summer vacation. He had been looking forward to this day for a long time. When he woke up early, he smiled at the sight of the bright sun shining through the window.

He went downstairs to have breakfast with his parents and siblings. On the table, there were toast, jam, and orange juice. Brad ate quickly because he was eager to start the day.

"I have many plans for this vacation," Brad said after finishing his breakfast.

His parents smiled. "What do you plan to do today?" his mother asked.

Brad replied, "I want to go to the park and play soccer with my friends. Then I'll go to the library to check out some books."

After breakfast, Brad put on his sneakers and left the house. First, he went to the park, where he played soccer with his friends. They ran and laughed a lot.

Then, Brad said goodbye to his friends and walked to the library. He loved reading and wanted to find new books for the vacation. At the library, he found several adventure books.

With his backpack full of books, Brad returned home. He sat in the garden and began to read. He was very happy and excited about all the adventures that awaited him during his vacation.

Chapter 40. Visiting the Grandparents

Chase and Michelle were very excited because they were going to visit their grandparents. They got into the car and started the journey. During the trip, they sang songs and played a game to see who could spot the most red cars.

When they arrived at their grandparents' house, they were greeted with hugs and kisses. "What a joy to see you!" said grandma. "We have prepared your favorite meal."

They went inside and sat at the table. There was chicken, rice, salad, and chocolate cake. Chase and Michelle ate very happily.

After eating, they went out to the garden to play. Grandpa showed them his garden full of flowers and plants. Chase and Michelle helped water the plants and picked some flowers.

"It's so much fun being here," said Chase while playing with the grandparents' dog.

"Yes, I love grandma and grandpa's house," replied Michelle.

They spent the afternoon playing and talking with their grandparents. At the end of the day, they were tired but very happy. "We have to come back soon!" said Chase.

"Of course," said grandma. "You are always welcome here."

They said goodbye to their grandparents and returned home. Chase and Michelle fell asleep quickly, dreaming of their next visit to their grandparents' house.

Exercises

Chapter 1. Day at School

Answer the following questions by choosing the correct option.

1. What did Emma have for breakfast?

a) Cereal

b) Toast with jam and warm milk

c) Bread with butter

2. Who prepared breakfast?

a) Emma

b) Her sister

c) Her mother

3. What was Emma's first class?

a) Natural sciences

b) Reading

c) Mathematics

4. What did Emma and her friends do during recess?

a) They played hopscotch and had a snack

b) They played soccer

c) They studied in the library

5. Who was waiting for Emma after school?

a) Her father

b) Her mother

c) Her grandmother

Chapter 2. A Walk in the Park

1. Olivia and her mother walked to the nearby ______.

a) park

b) beach

c) supermarket

2. They saw little children playing on the ______.

a) cars

b) swings

c) books

3. The mother pointed to a ______ climbing up the trunk of a large oak tree.

a) butterfly

b) squirrel

c) dog

4. Olivia watched the little _______ move nimbly.

a) flower

b) children

c) animal

5. The scent of spring _______ filled the fresh air.

a) flowers

b) fruits

c) leaves

Chapter 3. Shopping at the Supermarket

Read the following sentences and determine if they are true or false.

1. William bought green apples at the supermarket.

2. William chose to take chicken and sausages from the meat section.

3. In the dairy aisle, William bought milk, cheese, and strawberry yogurt.

4. William paid for his purchases with cash.

5. William was sad after shopping.

Chapter 4. Liam's Family

Connect the following parts of the sentences to form coherent phrases.

1. Liam has a family...

2. Noah is tall and...

3. Ava is a teacher and...

4. Sophia is a girl...

5. Abigail is Liam's grandmother and...

a) she always has a smile on her face.

b) small but happy.

c) has short black hair.

d) very energetic and curious.

e) an excellent cook.

Chapter 5. James's Birthday

Complete the sentences with the words provided. Words: friends, piñata, birthday, cake, gifts.

1. James is very excited because today is his ___________.

2. James's mother bought a big chocolate ___________ with frosting.

3. All of James' ___________ from school came to the party.

4. The guests gave him _____________ wrapped in shiny papers.

5. They played to break a _____________ full of candies.

Chapter 6. A Day at the Beach

Arrange the following words to form complete sentences.

1. at / beach / a / day / the

2. was / sand / the / hot / very

3. big / set / umbrella / up / parents / a

4. small / he / built / a / sandcastle

5. they / afternoon / spent / the / sunbathing

Chapter 7. At the Train Station

Arrange the sentences in the correct chronological order.

a) The family walks to the platform to wait for their train.

b) Amelia wakes up early and dresses in comfortable clothes.

c) Amelia and Daniel entertain themselves by counting the train cars.

d) The family hears a loud whistle and the train begins to move.

e) Dad buys the tickets at the counter.

Chapter 8. My Pet

Complete the sentences with the appropriate forms of the verbs.

1. Max (wag) ______________ his tail happily when I come home after school.

2. He (chase) ______________ a red ball all over the park.

3. Max (carry) ______________ a red plastic bone as his favorite toy.

4. Sometimes, he (hide) ______________ the bone under the furniture.

5. After playing, Max (curl up) ______________ in his little bed.

Chapter 9. A Rainy Day

Answer the following questions by choosing the correct option.

1. What type of day is it today?

a) Sunny

b) Cloudy

c) Rainy

2. Where did mom put the books and games?

a) In the living room

b) In the garden

c) In the garage

3. What does the narrator choose to do?

a) Play outside in the rain

b) Read a storybook

c) Play chess with Harper

4. What is mom doing while the children read and play?

a) Sleeping in her room

b) Watching TV

c) Cooking something delicious in the kitchen

5. How do the children feel at the end of the rainy day?

a) Bored

b) Happy to be together

c) Sad not to be able to go outside

Chapter 10. Dinner at Home

Complete the following sentences using the missing words.

1. Elijah was excited because he really likes being in the ______.

a) kitchen

b) living room

c) garden

2. At the supermarket, they bought _______ for the salad.

a) apples

b) potatoes and onions

c) lettuce, tomatoes, carrots, and cucumbers

3. Dad seasoned the chicken with _______, pepper, and a little lemon.

a) salt

b) sugar

c) flour

4. Mom cooked the rice in a _______ pot.

a) medium

b) large

c) small

5. Elijah helped to serve the salad and _______.

a) the soup

b) the rice

c) the vegetables

Chapter 11. Visit to the Zoo

Read the following sentences and determine if they are true or false.

1. Aiden and Jacob visited London Zoo one Saturday morning.

2. The first thing they saw were the lions resting under the sun.

3. Aiden said the elephants looked like walking houses.

4. The monkeys behaved as if they were children playing in a park.

5. Aiden watched fascinated as the tigers in the aviary.

Chapter 12. A Day in the Mountains

Connect the following parts of the sentences to form coherent phrases.

1. Logan and his family...

2. Logan packed...

3. Logan picked...

4. They enjoyed the view ...

5. They stayed a while longer...

a) some wildflowers.

b) of the majestic mountains.

c) decided to go hiking.

d) enjoying the scenery.

e) his backpack.

Chapter 13. My Best Friend

Complete the sentences with the words provided. Words: soccer, imagination, inseparable, adventures, bikes.

1. Alexander and I have been ___________ since we met at school.

2. We love playing ___________ and spend many afternoons practicing in the park.

3. We enjoy exploring the neighborhood in search of ___________.

4. We often ride our ___________ along the trails in the nearby forest.

5. We spend hours creating things with building blocks, letting our ___________ soar.

Chapter 14. The Neighborhood Party

Arrange the following words to form complete sentences.

1. party / started / the / dusk / at

2. have / time / a / together / good

3. my / are / specialty / they

4. the / of / rhythm / music / the

5. time / a / all / we / had / great

Chapter 15. The Doctor's Visit

Arrange the sentences in the correct chronological order.

a) Doctor Smith listened to Thomas's chest with the stethoscope.

b) Thomas and his dad arrived at the doctor's office.

c) Thomas stayed at home and followed the doctor's instructions.

d) Thomas's dad called the doctor's office and got an appointment.

e) The doctor gave Thomas a lollipop for being a good patient.

Chapter 16. The Soccer Match

Complete the sentences with the appropriate forms of the verbs.

1. Henry and his friends (gather) _____________ at the park to play soccer on Saturday afternoon.

2. They were very excited and full of energy, (form) _____________ the teams eagerly.

3. Right from the start, the match (be) _____________ intense.

4. Henry (mark) _____________ the field with rocks and backpacks before the game.

5. After the match, everyone (sit) ____________ on the grass, tired but happy.

Chapter 17. My Room

Answer the following questions by choosing the correct option.

1. What color are the walls in the room?

a) Light blue

b) White

c) Yellow

2. Where is the desk located?

a) Next to the bed

b) By the window

c) Across from the wardrobe

3. What is kept on the bedside table?

a) Clothes and shoes

b) A book and a reading lamp

c) Toys and figures

4. Where does the narrator sit to read or listen to music?

a) On the bed

b) In the wardrobe

c) In a comfortable chair in the corner

5. What does the narrator like most about their room?

a) The large wardrobe

b) The shelves with books

c) The feeling of tranquility it gives

Chapter 18. A Plane Journey

Complete the following sentences using the missing words.

1. Abigail was excited but also a bit ______.

a) nervous

b) happy

c) angry

2. At the London airport, there was a lot of people ______ .

a) eating

b) playing

c) coming and going

3. Abigail sat by the window and fastened the ______ .

a) seatbelt

b) gate

c) passport

4. Below them, the houses and streets looked tiny like ______.

a) cars

b) toys

c) buildings

5. Abigail felt like a ______ soaring through the sky.

a) plane

b) bird

c) boat

Chapter 19. My Spanish Class

Read the following sentences and determine if they are true or false.

1. The Spanish class teacher's name is Mrs. Brown.

2. There are twelve students in the class.

3. Scarlett is very good at pronunciation.

4. Spanish classes are on Mondays and Wednesdays.

5. They always start the class with a game in Spanish.

Chapter 20. The Library

Connect the following parts of the sentences to form coherent phrases.

1. John went to the library...

2. Mrs. Grace always...

3. First, he went to...

4. John sat down and...

5. The library is a...

a) started reading the pirate book.

b) the adventure section.

c) magical place for John.

d) on Saturday morning.

e) helps him find good books.

Chapter 21. An Afternoon at the Movies

Complete the sentences with the words provided. Words: seats, cinema, friends, popcorn, scenes.

1. Lily and her ___________ decided to go to the movies.

2. They bought ___________, sodas, and candies.

3. They found their ___________ and sat comfortably.

4. The movie was very exciting and had many action __________.

5. They left the __________ discussing their favorite scenes.

Chapter 22. The Music Festival

Arrange the following words to form complete sentences.

1. to / Alice / music / went / the / festival

2. band / a / was / first / the / concert / by / rock

3. bought / from / food / they / stalls / the

4. with / lit / lights / the / up / festival

5. it / incredible / was / experience / an

Chapter 23. A Bike Ride

Arrange the sentences in the correct chronological order.

a) They changed direction and took the dirt road.

b) They got on their bikes and started their adventure.

c) Freddie and his dad decided to go for a bike ride.

d) Freddie saw a dirt road that looked interesting.

e) They discovered a beautiful forest full of singing birds and small streams.

Chapter 24. Art Class

Complete the sentences with the appropriate forms of the verbs.

1. She (see) ______________ many paintings and brushes on the tables.

2. Julia (think) ______________ of the beach she visited with her family.

3. All the students (create) ______________ beautiful landscapes.

4. Mrs. White (walk) ______________ among the tables.

5. At the end of the class, everyone (show) ______________ their paintings.

Chapter 25. A Snowy Day

Answer the following questions by choosing the correct option.

1. What did David do first when he went out to the garden?

a) He made a snowman

b) He made snowballs

c) He played with Jack

2. What did David use for the snowman's nose?

a) A carrot

b) A stone

c) A button

3. Who arrived while David was making the snowman?

a) His mom

b) His brother

c) His friend Jack

4. What did David and Jack do with the snowman?

a) They put stones for the eyes

b) They put buttons for the mouth

c) They put a scarf on the snowman

5. What did David's mom give them when they went inside the house?

a) Cookies

b) Orange juice

c) Hot chocolate

Chapter 26. The History Museum

Complete the following sentences using the missing words.

1. Benjamin visited the history museum with his ______.

a) family

b) class

c) friend

2. Mr. Jones first took them to the _______ room.

a) ancient Egyptians

b) Middle Ages

c) dinosaurs

3. In the ancient Egyptians room, they saw mummies and _______.

a) pyramids

b) sarcophagi

c) castles

4. In the Middle Ages, castles served as _______.

a) fortresses

b) tombs

c) museums

5. At the end of the tour, Benjamin was _______.

a) tired

b) sad

c) happy

Chapter 27. My Favorite Breakfast

Read the following sentences and determine if they are true or false.

1. The narrator's favorite breakfast is vegan.

2. One banana is always added to breakfast.

3. The narrator adds fresh strawberries and blueberries.

4. The breakfast includes oats.

5. The breakfast never has chia seeds.

Chapter 28. A Day in the Countryside

Connect the following parts of the sentences to form coherent phrases.

1. Megan woke up early...

2. When they arrived at the countryside...

3. Megan and her family walked...

4. At noon, they sat...

5. Megan played with...

a) under a large tree for lunch.

b) Megan saw many animals.

c) and was very excited.

d) her little brother.

e) along a trail in the forest.

Chapter 29. The Dentist Visit

Complete the sentences with the words provided. Words: toys, chair, dentist, teeth, toothbrush.

1. Charlie an appointment with the _______________.

2. In the waiting room, Charlie saw some _______________.

3. Dr. Davis explained everything while Charlie sat in the big _______________.

4. Dr. Davis said that Charlie's _______________ are in great shape.

5. After the check-up, Dr. Davis gave Charlie a new _______________.

Chapter 30. The Book Fair

Arrange the following words to form complete sentences.

1. park / the / fair / a / in / large / was

2. there / many / with / colors / bright / books / were

3. about / saw / Steve / dinosaurs / book / a

4. is / learn / important / new / it / a / things / to

5. adventure / great / is / a / reading

Chapter 31. A Walk Downtown

Arrange the sentences in the correct chronological order.

a) Mike went to a café.

b) Mike saw his friend Noah.

c) Mike decided to visit a museum.

d) Mike walked through the streets filled with shops.

e) Mike visited a bookstore.

Chapter 32. A Day at the Aquarium

Complete the sentences with the appropriate forms of the verbs.

1. Kate and her classmates (decide) _____________ to go to the aquarium.

2. They (to go) _____________ straight to the large tanks.

3. Kate's friends (begin) _____________ naming the different types of fish.

4. They (learn) _____________ about the different types of sharks.

5. They had (have) _____________ an incredible day at the aquarium.

Chapter 33. The New Year's Eve Party

Answer the following questions by choosing the correct option.

1. What were Miley and Andrew doing before their friends arrived?

a) Sleeping

b) Decorating and preparing the music

c) Cooking

2. Who brought food and drinks to the party?

a) Miley and Andrew

b) The neighbors

c) Nicole, Tyler, Susan, and Justin

3. What did everyone do just before midnight?

a) Went to sleep

b) Watched the countdown on TV

c) Went out to the garden

4. What did everyone do at midnight?

a) Ate grapes and hugged each other

b) Went home

c) Turned on the lights

5. How did Miley and Andrew feel at the end of the party?

a) Sad

b) Tired

c) Very happy

Chapter 34. Music Class

Complete the following sentences using the missing words.

1. Sarah was very excited about her _______ class.

a) math

b) music

c) science

2. Mr. Moore was going to teach them how to play the _______.

a) guitar

b) drums

c) flute

3. Mr. Moore showed the students how to _______ the flute.

a) hold

b) clean

c) paint

4. Sarah tried to follow Mr. Moore's _______.

a) rules

b) instructions

c) questions

5. At the end of the class, all the students were able to _______ a song.

a) play

b) draw

c) dance

Chapter 35. The New Job

Read the following sentences and determine if they are true or false.

1. Daniel arrived late on his first day of work.

2. Daniel's boss is named Mr. Wilson.

3. Sandra is a coworker who helped Daniel.

4. During the morning, Daniel worked on his first project.

5. At the end of the day, Daniel went home happy.

Chapter 36. A Day at the Gym

Connect the following parts of the sentences to form coherent phrases.

1. Alex woke up early with...

2. A friendly instructor greeted him...

3. Alex decided to start with

4. Alex moved on to lifting weights...

5. Alex felt tired...

a) a light warm-up.

b) a determination in mind.

c) but satisfied.

d) and guided him around the gym.

e) and doing strength exercises.

Chapter 37. The Photography Workshop

Complete the sentences with the words provided. Words: taking, learning, photography, happy, nature.

1. When Camila saw the advertisement about for _______________ workshops, she decided to sign up.

2. Camila was happy to be _______________ something new.

3. Camila discovered that she liked to photograph _______________ and small details.

4. Camila felt _______________ and proud when she knew that she loved photography.

5. Camila imagined traveling to distant places and _______________

photos.

Chapter 38. The Dance Class

Arrange the following words to form complete sentences.

1. to / a / dance / enroll / Gary / decided / in / class

2. the / foot / we / right / forward / move

3. time / great / everyone / was / a / having

4. you / improving / each / are / step / with

5. Miller / them / tips / mrs. / gave / some

Chapter 39. The First Day of Vacation

Arrange the sentences in the correct chronological order.

a) Brad ate toast and jam for breakfast.

b) Brad sat in the garden and began to read.

c) Brad played soccer with his friends in the park.

d) Brad walked to the library to check out some books.

e) Brad woke up early and smiled when he saw the sun.

Chapter 40. Visiting the Grandparents

Complete the sentences with the appropriate forms of the verbs.

1. Chase and Michelle (to be) ____________ excited to visit

their grandparents.

2. During the trip they (sing) ______________ songs and played a game.

3. Chase and Michelle (eat) ______________ very happily.

4. They (to spend) ______________ the afternoon playing and talking with their grandparents.

5. They (to say) ______________ goodbye to their grandparents and returned home.

Solutions

Chapter 1. Day at School

1. b) Toast with jam and warm milk

2. c) Her mother

3. c) Mathematics

4. a) They played hopscotch and had a snack

5. b) Her mother

Chapter 2. A Walk in the Park

1. a) park

2. b) swings

3. b) squirrel

4. c) animal

5. a) flowers

Chapter 3. Shopping at the Supermarket

1. False (William bought red apples.)

2. True

3. True

4. False (William paid with his debit card.)

5. False (William left the supermarket happy.)

Chapter 4. Liam's Family

1. b) Liam has a family small but happy.

2. c) Noah is tall and has short black hair.

3. e) Ava is a teacher and an excellent cook.

4. d) Sophia is a girl very energetic and curious.

5. a) Abigail is Liam's grandmother and she always has a smile on her face.

Chapter 5. James's Birthday

1. birthday

2. cake

3. friends

4. gifts

5. piñata

Chapter 6. A Day at the Beach

1. A day at the beach.

2. The sand was very hot.

3. Parents set up a big umbrella.

4. He built a small sandcastle.

5. They spent the afternoon sunbathing.

Chapter 7. At the Train Station

1. b) Amelia wakes up early and dresses in comfortable clothes.

2. e) Dad buys the tickets at the counter.

3. a) The family walks to the platform to wait for their train.

4. c) Amelia and Daniel entertain themselves by counting the train cars.

5. d) The family hears a loud whistle and the train begins to move.

Chapter 8. My Pet

1. wags

2. chases

3. carries

4. hides

5. curls up

Chapter 9. A Rainy Day

1. c) Rainy

2. a) In the living room

3. b) Read a storybook

4. c) Cooking something delicious in the kitchen

5. b) Happy to be together

Chapter 10. Dinner at Home

1. a) kitchen

2. c) lettuce, tomatoes, carrots, and cucumbers

3. a) salt

4. b) large

5. b) the rice

Chapter 11. Visit to the Zoo

1. False (Aiden and Jacob visited London Zoo one Sunday morning.)

2. True

3. True

4. True

5. False (Aiden watched fascinated as the parrots in the aviary.)

Chapter 12. A Day in the Mountains

1. c) Logan and his family decided to go hiking.

2. e) Logan packed his backpack.

3. a) Logan picked some wildflowers.

4. b) They enjoyed the view of the majestic mountains.

5. d) They stayed a while longer enjoying the scenery.

Chapter 13. My Best Friend

1. inseparable

2. soccer

3. adventures

4. bikes

5. imagination

Chapter 14. The Neighborhood Party

1. The party started at dusk.

2. Have a good time together.

3. They are my specialty.

4. The rhythm of the music.

5. We all had a great time.

Chapter 15. The Doctor's Visit

1. d) Thomas's dad called the doctor's office and got an appointment.

2. b) Thomas and his dad arrived at the doctor's office.

3. a) Doctor Smith listened to Thomas's chest with the stethoscope.

4. e) The doctor gave Thomas a lollipop for being a good patient.

5. c) Thomas stayed at home and followed the doctor's instructions.

Chapter 16. The Soccer Match

1. gathered

2. forming

3. was

4. marked

5. sat

Chapter 17. My Room

1. a) Light blue

2. b) By the window

3. b) A book and a reading lamp

4. c) In a comfortable chair in the corner

5. c) The feeling of tranquility it gives

Chapter 18. A Plane Journey

1. a) nervous

2. c) coming and going

3. a) seatbelt

4. b) toys

5. b) bird

Chapter 19. My Spanish Class

1. False (The Spanish class teacher's name is Mrs. Johnson.)

2. False (There are ten students in the class.)

3. True

4. False (Spanish classes are on Tuesdays and Thursdays.)

5. True

Chapter 20. The Library

1. d) John went to the library on Saturday morning.

2. e) Mrs. Grace always helps him find good books.

3. b) First, he went to the adventure section.

4. a) John sat down and started reading the pirate book.

5. c) The library is a magical place for John.

Chapter 21. An Afternoon at the Movies

1. friends

2. popcorn

3. seats

4. scenes

5. cinema

Chapter 22. The Music Festival

1. Alice went to the music festival.

2. The first concert was by a rock band.

3. They bought food from the stalls.

4. The festival lit up with lights.

5. It was an incredible experience.

Chapter 23. A Bike Ride

1. c) Freddie and his dad decided to go for a bike ride.

2. b) They got on their bikes and started their adventure.

3. d) Freddie saw a dirt road that looked interesting.

4. a) They changed direction and took the dirt road.

5. e) They discovered a beautiful forest full of singing birds and small streams.

Chapter 24. Art Class

1. saw

2. thought

3. created

4. walked

5. showed

Chapter 25. A Snowy Day

1. b) He made snowballs

2. a) A carrot

3. c) His friend Jack

4. b) They put buttons for the mouth

5. c) Hot chocolate

Chapter 26. The History Museum

1. b) class

2. c) dinosaurs

3. b) sarcophagi

4. a) fortresses

5. c) happy

Chapter 27. My Favorite Breakfast

1. True

2. False (Sometimes, two bananas are used if very hungry.)

3. True

4. True

5. False (Sometimes, chia seeds are also added on top.)

Chapter 28. A Day in the Countryside

1. c) Megan woke up early and was very excited.

2. b) When they arrived at the countryside, Megan saw many animals.

3. e) Megan and her family walked along a trail in the forest.

4. a) At noon, they sat under a large tree for lunch.

5. d) Megan played with her little brother.

Chapter 29. The Dentist Visit

1. dentist

2. toys

3. chair

4. teeth

5. toothbrush

Chapter 30. The Book Fair

1. The fair was in a large park.

2. There were many books with bright colors.

3. Steve saw a book about dinosaurs.

4. It is important to learn new things.

5. Reading is a great adventure.

Chapter 31. A Walk Downtown

1. d) Mike walked through the streets filled with shops.

2. e) Mike visited a bookstore.

3. b) Mike saw his friend Noah.

4. a) Mike went to a café.

5. c) Mike decided to visit a museum.

Chapter 32. A Day at the Aquarium

1. decided

2. went

3. began

4. learned

5. had

Chapter 33. The New Year's Eve Party

1. b) Decorating and preparing the music

2. c) Nicole, Tyler, Susan, and Justin

3. b) Watched the countdown on TV

4. a) Ate grapes and hugged each other

5. c) Very happy

Chapter 34. La Clase de Música

1. b) music

2. c) flute

3. a) hold

4. b) instructions

5. a) play

Chapter 35. The New Job

1. False (Daniel arrived early on his first day of work.)

2. True

3. True

4. False (In the afternoon, Daniel worked on his first project.)

5. True

Chapter 36. A Day at the Gym

1. b) Alex woke up early with a determination in mind.

2. d) A friendly instructor greeted him and guided him around the gym.

3. a) Alex decided to start with a light warm-up.

4. e) Alex moved on to lifting weights and doing strength exercises.

5. c) Alex felt tired but satisfied.

Chapter 37. The Photography Workshop

1. photography

2. learning

3. nature

4. happy

5. taking

Chapter 38. The Dance Class

1. Gary decided to enroll in a dance class.

2. We move the right foot forward.

3. Everyone was having a great time.

4. You are improving with each step.

5. Mrs. Miller gave them some tips.

Chapter 39. The First Day of Vacation

1. e) Brad woke up early and smiled when he saw the sun.

2. a) Brad ate toast and jam for breakfast.

3. c) Brad played soccer with his friends in the park.

4. d) Brad walked to the library to check out some books.

5. b) Brad sat in the garden and began to read.

Chapter 40. Visiting the Grandparents

1. were

2. sang

3. ate

4. spent

5. said

www.ingramcontent.com/pod-product-compliance
Lightning Source LLC
Chambersburg PA
CBHW072238150726
48002CB00005B/2153